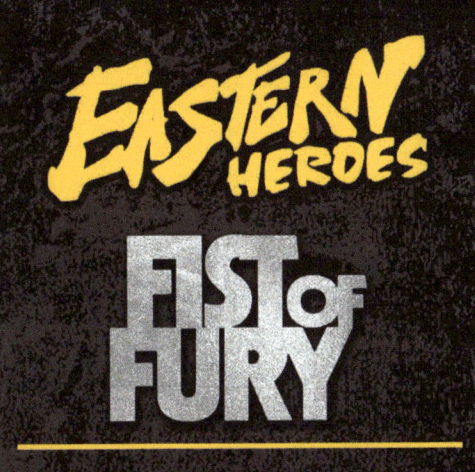

Published by Eastern Heroes Publishing
Produced by Rick Baker

Designer (cover and Interior layout)
Tim Hollingsworth
Instagram: 79_design

Printing: Ingramspark

Contributors:

UK
Rick Baker
Simon Pritchard
Mike Nesbitt

USA
John Negron
Jason McNeil

GERMANY
Thomas Gross

All rights reserved. No part of this publication may be reproduced or transmitted in any or by any means, graphic, electronic or mechanical, including photocopying, recording, taping or any information storage and retrieval system, without prior written permission of the publisher.
© 2023 Eastern Heroes.

EDITORIAL

Welcome to the latest Collector's Edition of our magazine, celebrating the unparalleled legacy of the one and only Bruce Lee. As we embark on this journey through the world of martial arts, we invite you to immerse yourself in the pages of this special volume dedicated to Bruce Lee's timeless masterpiece, Fist of Fury.

Martial Arts Icon: Fist of Fury – Bruce Lee's Masterpiece. Join us as we revisit this cinematic gem, dissecting its themes, choreography, and cultural significance that continue to resonate with audiences worldwide.

Next, we delve into the legacy of Chen Zhen, the iconic character portrayed by Bruce Lee in Fist of Fury. Discover how this character has transcended generations, inspiring countless martial artists and filmmakers to this day.

For collectors and enthusiasts alike, we offer an exclusive look into John Negron's Bruce Lee Fist of Fury Memorabilia Collection. Prepare to be awestruck by rare artefacts and cherished memorabilia that capture the essence of Bruce Lee's martial arts legacy.

German collector Thomas Gross shares part one of his rare Fist of Fury memorabilia collections, providing a glimpse into the global fascination with Bruce Lee's legacy.

Furthermore, we unveil the legacy of Mike Nesbitt's "Bruce Lee Column – Real or Fake: Chinese Gung Fu," shedding light on the myths and misconceptions surrounding Bruce Lee's martial arts philosophy.

As if that wasn't enough, feast your eyes on the Fist of Fury Photo gallery, where stunning images from the film and behind-the-scenes moments come to life, transporting you into the heart of the action.

Thank you for joining us on this journey. Let's celebrate the legend of Bruce Lee together.

Keeping the faith

Rick Baker

Rick Baker

CONTENTS

2. Fist Of Fury: A Martial Arts masterpiece

10. Chen Zhen: The enduring legacy of Bruce Lee's Fist Of Fury

15. Unveling the Legacy

26. Real or Fake: The Bruce Lee Column By Michael Nesbitt

31. Fist Of Fury Photo Gallery

49. Memoribilia with Thomas Gross

82. The Gatekeeper of Bruce Lee's Legacy (part 2) with Jeff Chinn

89. John Negron's Memorabilia

BRUCE LEE'S
FIST OF FURY
A MARTIAL ARTS MASTERPIECE
By Rick Baker

Bruce Lee's "Fist of Fury," also known as "The Chinese Connection," stands as one of the most iconic martial arts films in cinema history. Released in 1972, this classic showcases Bruce Lee's exceptional skills as a martial artist, actor, and director. The film not only left an indelible mark on the martial arts genre but also played a crucial role in catapulting Bruce Lee to international stardom. This article delves into the background, production, and impact of "Fist of Fury."

"Fist of Fury" was Bruce Lee's second major film after "The Big Boss" (1971). Directed by Lo Wei, the film was released in Hong Kong in March 1972. The story is set in Shanghai during the early 20th century, depicting the struggles of the Chinese people against Japanese oppression. Bruce Lee plays the role of Chen Zhen, a character he would later portray in various adaptations by other filmmakers.

The plot revolves around Chen Zhen seeking justice for the death of his martial arts teacher, Huo Yuanjia, who was poisoned by the Japanese school. Chen infiltrates the Japanese martial arts school, taking on numerous opponents in a quest for retribution. The film's narrative is tightly woven around themes of honour, national pride, and the indomitable spirit of resistance.

Cultural and Historical Context

"Fist of Fury" is deeply rooted in the historical context of the Japanese occupation of China during the early 20th century. The film reflects the sentiment of Chinese resistance against foreign oppression, making it a powerful cultural artefact. Bruce Lee's portrayal of a defiant and skilled martial artist resonated with audiences, creating a sense of national pride and empowerment. Bruce Lee's performance in "Fist of Fury" solidified his status as a martial arts icon. His unparalleled skills and charisma brought a new level of authenticity to on-screen combat. The film showcased his philosophy of martial arts as a means of self-expression and self-improvement, emphasizing speed, precision, and adaptability.

Impact on Martial Arts Cinema

Choreography and Realism: One of the key elements that set "Fist of Fury" apart was its ground-breaking choreography, which elevated the standard for fight sequences in martial arts films. Bruce Lee, who was deeply involved in the choreography process, insisted on realism and authenticity in every move. The fight scenes were meticulously designed to showcase Lee's speed, precision, and innovative martial arts techniques. This emphasis on realistic combat was a departure from the stylized and theatrical fight scenes of previous martial arts films, contributing to the film's unique appeal. Notably, the iconic nunchaku scene in "Fist of Fury" became legendary, showcasing Bruce Lee's mastery of this unconventional weapon. The intricate choreography and Lee's unparalleled proficiency with the nunchaku left an indelible mark on the genre, inspiring countless martial artists and filmmakers to explore new and dynamic fighting styles.

The success of "Fist of Fury" marked a turning point for martial arts cinema. It demonstrated that martial arts films could not only be commercially successful but also critically acclaimed for their technical excellence. The film's influence extended far beyond its initial release, shaping the trajectory of martial arts movies for decades to come. In the wake of "Fist of Fury," a wave of martial arts films emerged collectively referred to as the "Kung Fu boom." Filmmakers sought to replicate the success of Bruce Lee's films by incorporating

similar themes of honour, revenge, and exceptional martial arts skills. These movies often featured charismatic martial artists who, like Bruce Lee, were not only skilled fighters but also possessed a unique screen presence.

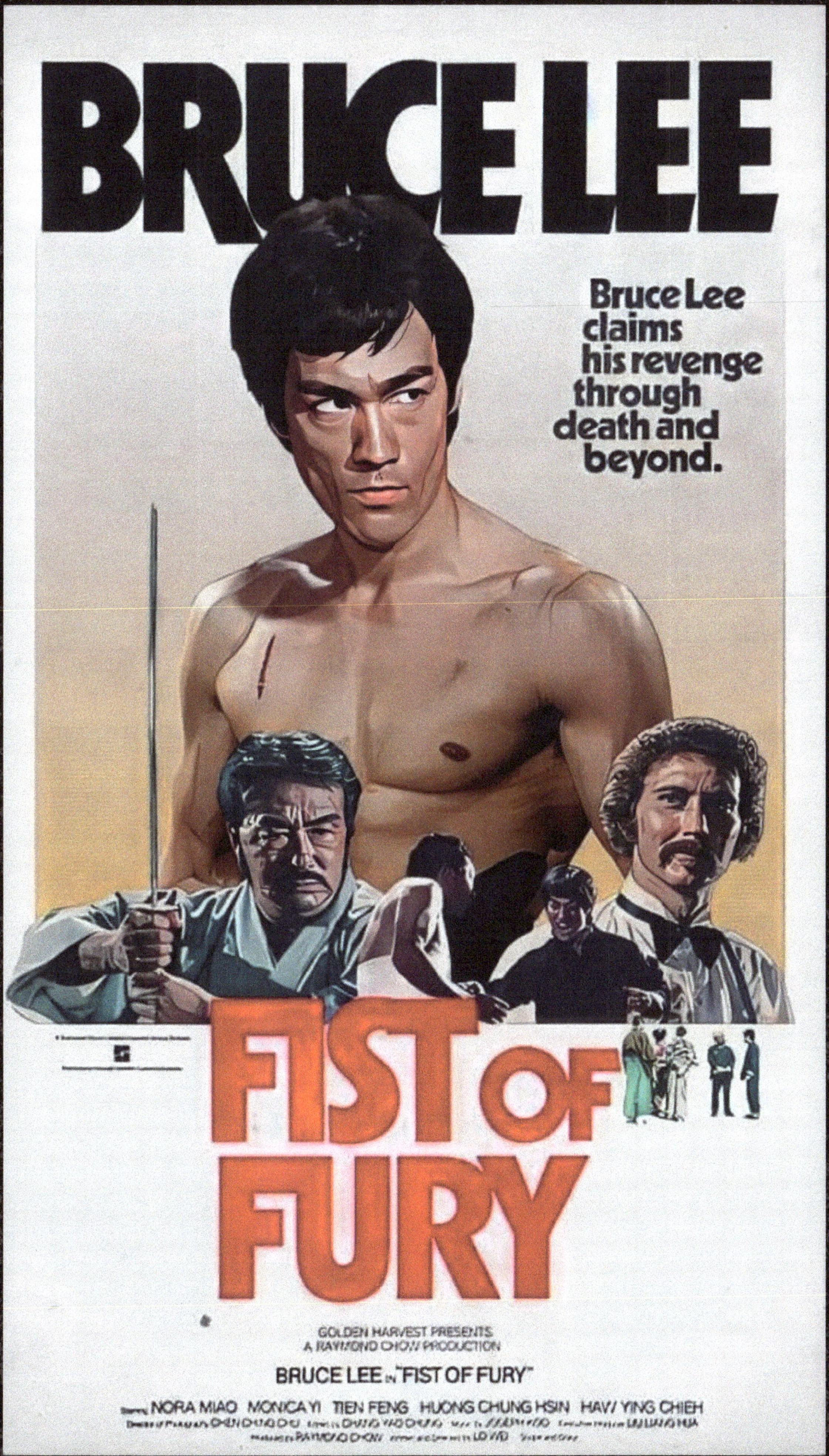

The Infiltration of Asian Martial Artists in Hollywood:

Following the success of Bruce Lee's films, particularly "Fist of Fury," Hollywood began to recognize the appeal of Asian martial arts stars and the potential of incorporating martial arts themes into mainstream cinema. Bruce Lee's ability to bridge the cultural gap and captivate audiences worldwide opened the door for other Asian martial artists to make their mark in Hollywood.

Jackie Chan, often regarded as one of the greatest action stars in the world, emerged as a prominent figure in Hollywood during the 1980s and 1990s. Chan's unique blend of martial arts, comedy, and stunts brought a fresh and entertaining dimension to the genre. His breakthrough in Hollywood, marked by films like "Rumble in the Bronx" (1995) and "Rush Hour" (1998), solidified his status as an international superstar.

Jet Li, another martial arts sensation, transitioned from his successful career in Hong Kong cinema to Hollywood. Li's Hollywood debut in "Lethal Weapon 4" (1998) and

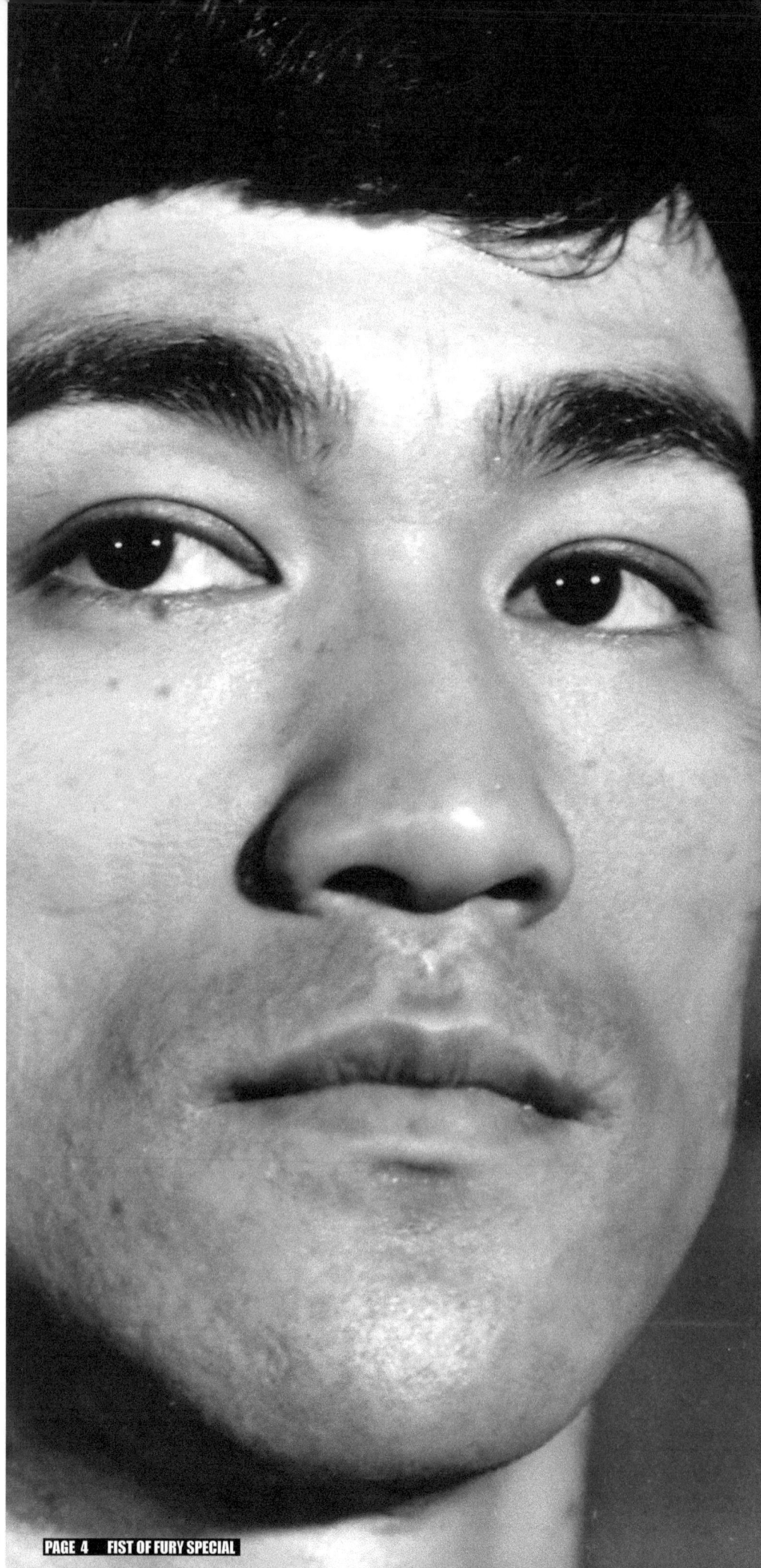

subsequent roles in films like "Romeo Must Die" (2000) and "The One" (2001) showcased his martial arts prowess and contributed to the growing influence of Asian martial artists in mainstream American cinema.

Martial Arts Choreography Across Genres

The integration of martial arts choreography became a defining feature of Hollywood's action repertoire. Martial arts were no longer confined to traditional kung fu films; they permeated various genres, from action blockbusters to fantasy and science fiction. Films like "The Matrix" (1999) directed by the Wachowskis, took martial arts choreography to new heights. Choreographer Yuen Woo-ping, renowned for his work in Hong Kong cinema, collaborated with Hollywood filmmakers to create gravity-defying fight sequences that left audiences in awe. The success of "The Matrix" further emphasized the global appeal of martial arts-inspired action, prompting other filmmakers to seek out Asian choreographers and martial artists for their productions.

Cultural Exchange and Impact

The influx of Asian martial artists into Hollywood marked a significant cultural exchange. Martial arts, once considered niche, became a universal language in cinema, breaking down cultural barriers and fostering a greater understanding and appreciation for Asian culture. The success of these films demonstrated that martial arts transcend borders, resonating with audiences worldwide. Moreover, the collaboration between Asian and Western filmmakers led to the exchange of ideas and techniques, enriching the cinematic landscape. Hollywood's embrace of martial arts not only broadened the scope of action films but also contributed to the evolution of fight choreography and the integration of diverse martial arts styles.

Bruce Lee's Global Legacy

Bruce Lee's influence on the global perception of martial arts was revolutionary. He challenged stereotypes, breaking down racial barriers and showcasing the philosophy and discipline behind martial arts. Lee's charismatic on-screen presence and his dedication to promoting martial arts as a way of life resonated with audiences worldwide, transcending cultural boundaries. Beyond film, Bruce Lee's legacy has endured through the establishment of his martial art philosophy, Jeet Kune Do, and his writings

on martial arts and personal development. His impact on popular culture extends to the realms of fashion, philosophy, and fitness, making him an enduring and inspirational figure across generations.

Challenging Stereotypes and Breaking down Racial Barriers

Bruce Lee's impact on the global perception of martial arts went beyond the silver screen, as he played a pivotal role in challenging stereotypes and breaking down racial barriers. At a time when Asian actors were often relegated to stereotypical roles in Hollywood, Bruce Lee's charisma and exceptional martial arts skills defied preconceived notions. His success in leading roles not only shattered racial stereotypes but also opened doors for Asian actors in the film industry.

Lee's iconic roles in films like "Fist of Fury" and "Enter the Dragon" showcased a strong, confident Asian protagonist, challenging the prevailing stereotypes of Asians as meek

or submissive. The on-screen representation of a powerful, skilled martial artist helped reshape perceptions of Asians in Western media, fostering a more nuanced and positive understanding of Asian cultures.

Promoting Philosophy and Discipline

Bruce Lee's dedication to promoting martial arts extended beyond physical prowess; it encompassed a philosophy that transcended the confines of the dojo. Lee's own martial art philosophy, known as, Jeet Kune Do, emphasized practicality, efficiency, and directness. It rejected rigid traditional forms, encouraging practitioners to absorb what is useful and discard what is not, promoting a fluid and adaptable approach to combat. Jeet Kune Do became a guiding philosophy for martial artists seeking a more dynamic and personalized approach to their training. Beyond the martial arts community, Lee's philosophy found resonance in various fields, including business, philosophy, and personal development. His emphasis on adaptability and self-expression inspired individuals to approach challenges with an open mind and a willingness to evolve.

Writings on Martial Arts and Personal Development

Bruce Lee's legacy as a martial artist and philosopher is preserved through his extensive writings on martial arts and personal development. His books, such as "Tao of Jeet Kune Do" and "Bruce Lee's Fighting Method," became essential texts for martial artists worldwide, offering insights into his philosophies, training methods, and life principles. In addition to martial arts, Lee explored broader themes of personal growth, self-discovery, and the pursuit of excellence. His writings transcended the boundaries of

martial arts literature, resonating with readers seeking inspiration and guidance in various aspects of life. The enduring popularity of Bruce Lee's written works attests to the timeless wisdom embedded in his teachings.

Impact on Popular Culture

Bruce Lee's influence extends into the realms of fashion, philosophy, and fitness, making him a multifaceted cultural icon. His distinctive style, both on and off-screen, left an indelible mark on fashion trends. The iconic yellow jumpsuit from "Game of Death" became a symbol of martial arts chic, and his signature hairstyle and casual attire influenced fashion choices around the world. Beyond aesthetics, Bruce Lee's philosophical teachings permeated popular culture. His quotes, such as "Be like water," became ubiquitous in motivational literature, inspiring individuals to be adaptable and resilient. The fusion of Eastern philosophy with Western practicality became a hallmark of Lee's influence on a global scale.

Conclusion

Bruce Lee's global legacy is a testament to his multifaceted impact on various facets of culture and society. From challenging racial stereotypes to shaping martial arts philosophy, his influence is far-reaching and enduring. Through his films, writings, and iconic presence, Bruce Lee continues to inspire generations, leaving an indelible mark on the global perception of martial arts and personal development. His legacy goes beyond the confines of time, making him an everlasting source of inspiration for those seeking excellence in both physical and philosophical pursuits.

CHEN ZHEN
陳真
The Enduring Legacy of Bruce Lee's Fist of Fury

By Rick Baker

While "Enter the Dragon" may stand as Bruce Lee's most significant movie, it is the character Chen Zhen from "Fist of Fury" that holds the utmost importance in the martial arts legend's career. Directed by Lo Wei and released in 1972, "Fist of Fury" marked Lee's second foray into martial arts cinema, following his breakthrough role in 1971's "The Big Boss."

In "Fist of Fury," Bruce Lee brings to life Chen Zhen, a Chinese martial artist returning home to discover the tragic demise of his kung fu master, Huo Yuanjia. The narrative unfolds as students from his school face harassment from Japanese fighters who disparage the Chinese. Initially advised to endure the humiliation, Chen Zhen learns that the Japanese were responsible for his master's death, prompting him to employ his formidable kung fu skills in retaliation. Despite emerging victorious in the ensuing battle, Chen Zhen's tale takes a tragic turn when confronted by a line of Japanese soldiers, ending the film with an impending sense of doom.

While "Fist of Fury" is a work of fiction, the death of Huo Yuanjia was a historical event, sparking speculation about the character's inspiration being loosely based on Huo Yuanjia's student, Liu Zhensheng. Following this film, Bruce Lee went on to create "Way of the Dragon" and "Enter the Dragon," both highly successful ventures. However, it is Chen Zhen who stands out as a character leaving an indelible mark on kung fu cinema.

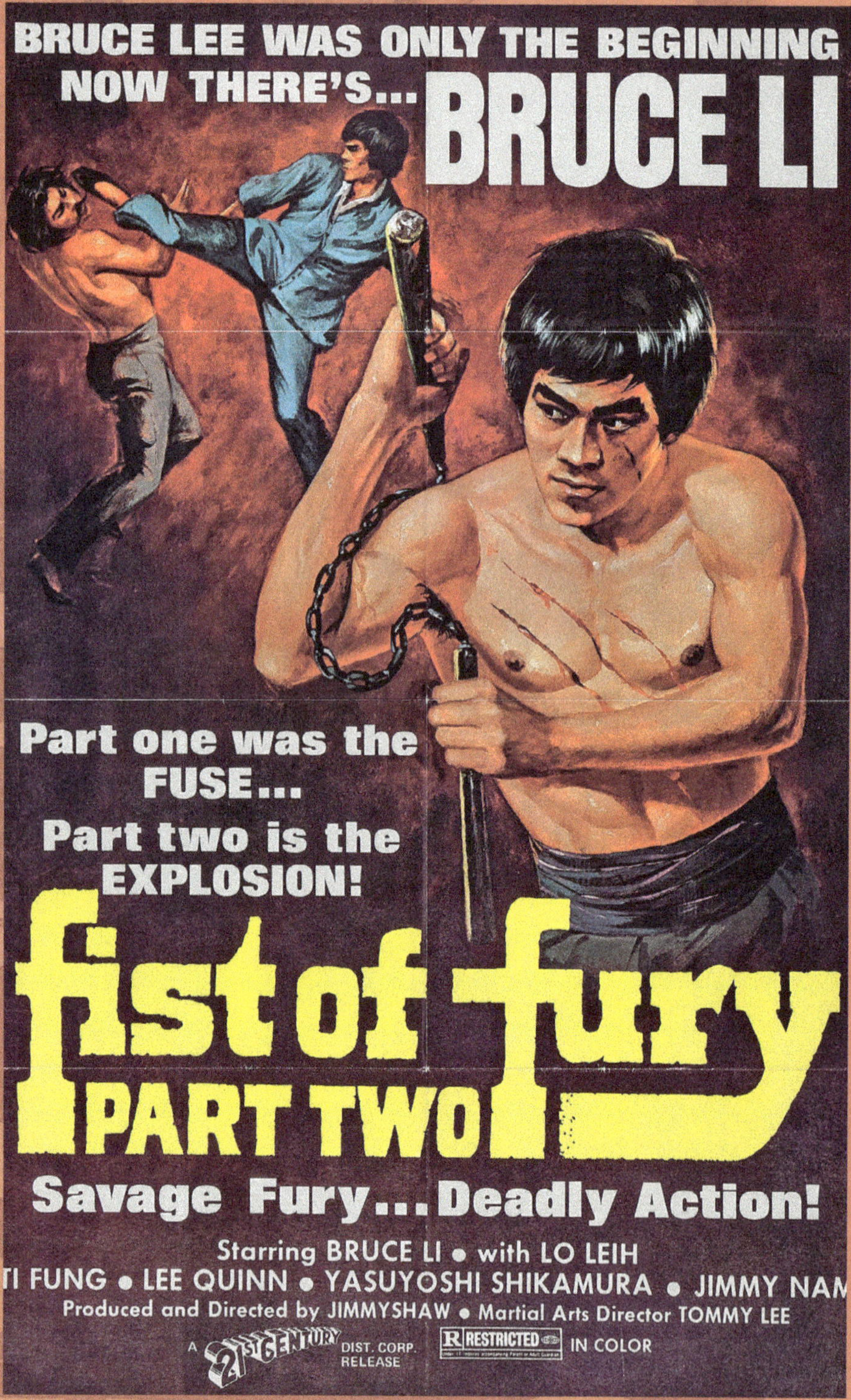

Chen Zhen's enduring legacy is rooted in the character's representation of Chinese pride and nationalism. "Fist of Fury" is a cinematic homage to Chinese heritage, portraying a protagonist unapologetically proud of his roots. By daring to stand against oppressive Japanese antagonists, Chen Zhen became an iconic symbol of Chinese patriotism, endearing him to audiences worldwide.

Chen Zhen's significance transcends his initial portrayal, as evidenced by subsequent cinematic adaptations. "New Fist of Fury" cast Jackie Chan in a role reminiscent of Bruce Lee's Chen Zhen, marking Chan's first leading role. Direct sequels to the original "Fist of Fury" were also produced, featuring Bruce Lee look-alikes.

Moreover, the character of Chen Zhen has been rejuvenated by martial arts luminaries Jet Li and Donnie Yen. In 1994, Jet Li starred in a high-profile remake titled "Fist of Legend," acclaimed as one of the best kung fu films of the decade. Even in the 2000s, Bruce Lee's Chen Zhen remains a popular figure, inspiring television shows and a 2010 adaptation where Donnie Yen portrayed a superheroic version in "Legend of the Fist: Return of Chen Zhen," staying true to the original film's themes.

Bruce Lee's "Fist of Fury" and the character of Chen Zhen continue to resonate, underscoring their cultural impact and enduring influence on the martial arts genre.

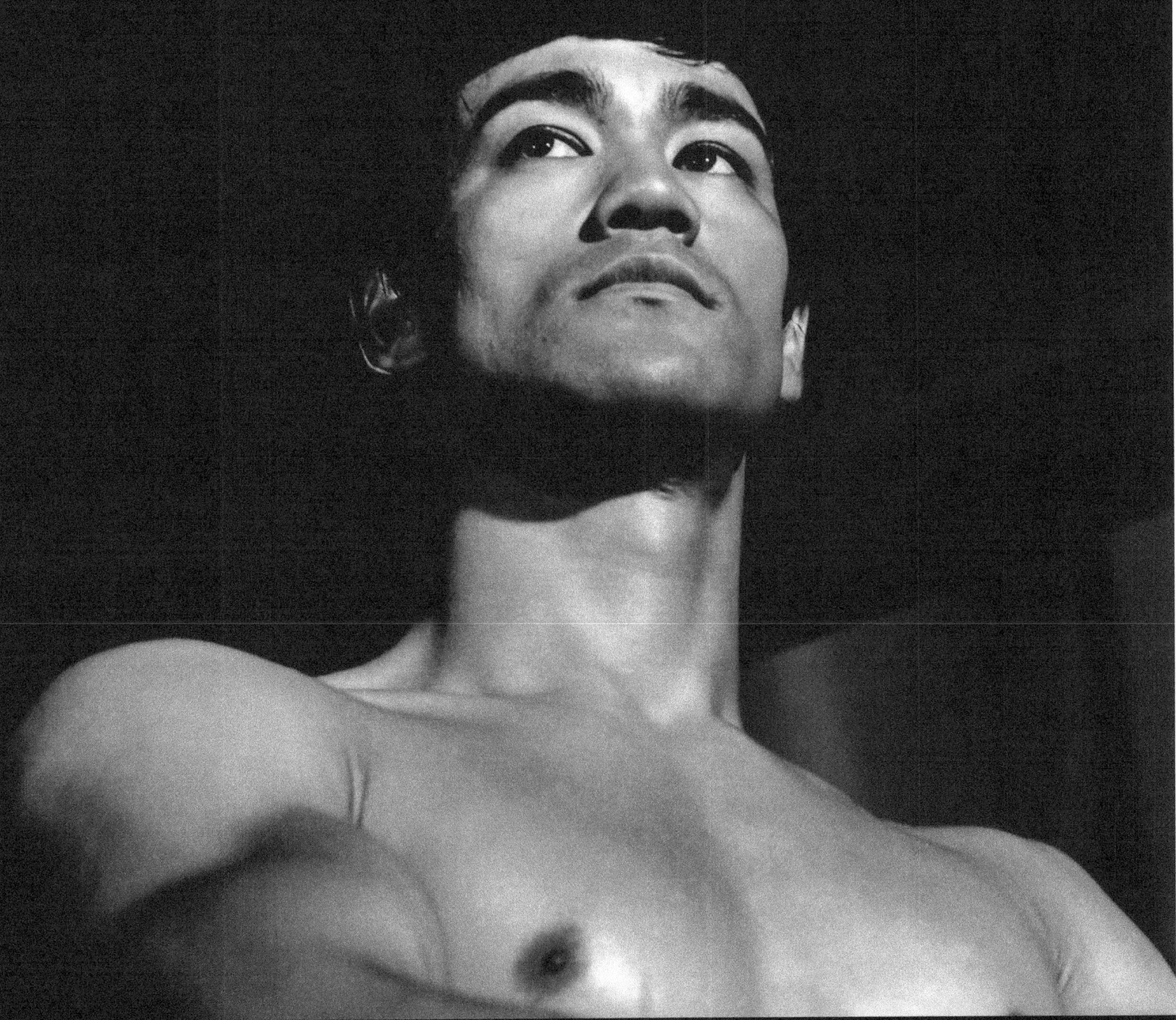

EMBARKING ON THE MARTIAL ARTS ODYSSEY
UNVEILING THE LEGACY OF
FIST OF FURY

Released in 1972, "Fist of Fury" directed by Lo Wei and produced by Raymond Chow, is a monumental martial arts film that etched itself into cinematic history. Let's delve into riveting facts about this iconic Bruce Lee masterpiece, from its groundbreaking impact on the film industry to the mesmerizing details behind its intense fight sequences.

Martial Arts Maestro: Bruce Lee Takes the Lead: Global Stardom: Bruce Lee, the lead actor and martial arts choreographer, showcased exceptional skills that propelled him to international stardom.

Setting the Stage: The film unfolds in 1930s Shanghai during the Japanese occupation, revolving around Chen Zhen seeking justice for his master's death.

Schools of Strife: "Fist of Fury" portrays a fierce rivalry between Jingwu and a Japanese Karate school, with Bruce Lee's character becoming a symbol of resistance.

Cinematic Triumphs: Box Office Records and Impact Box Office Triumph: Grossing over HK$3.2 million upon release, "Fist of Fury" shattered records and became one of Hong Kong's highest-grossing films.

Influence and Inspiration: The film inspired a wave of martial arts movies, setting new standards for action choreography and influencing future actors and filmmakers.

Franchise Expansion: Success led to sequels and spin-offs, expanding the Fist of Fury franchise and entertaining martial arts enthusiasts globally.

Cultural Milestones: Beyond Borders. Globalization of Martial Arts Cinema: Particularly popular in Asian countries, "Fist of Fury" played a vital role in globalizing martial arts cinema, showcasing Asian talent worldwide.

Iconic Imagery: The striking poster featuring Bruce Lee in a fighting pose became an iconic image, referenced in various forms of media.

Musical Intensity: Joseph Koo's impactful soundtrack added depth to action sequences, perfectly complementing on-screen martial arts battles.

Bruce Lee's Influence: Nunchaku Mastery and Hollywood Awaits. The film showcases Bruce Lee's nunchaku fighting style, inspiring martial artists worldwide with his fluid and precise movements.

Hollywood Calling: "Fist of Fury" paved the way for Bruce Lee's Hollywood career, catching the attention of international filmmakers and leading to his iconic role in "Enter the Dragon."

Enduring Legacy: Timeless Classic and Cultural Impact. Philosophy of Martial Arts: Bruce Lee's martial arts philosophy, emphasizing honour and self-discipline, is woven into the character of Chen Zhen.

Wing Chun Showcase: The film features Wing Chun, a style of kung Fu, with Bruce Lee's display of impressive techniques popularizing the martial art worldwide.

Fight Against Discrimination: A powerful scene symbolizes the fight against racial discrimination, drawing attention to the struggles faced by Chinese immigrants.

Pop Culture Phenomenon: Parodies and Adaptations. "Fist of Fury" left an indelible mark on popular culture, with numerous parodies and references across films, TV shows, and comics.

Imitators and Clones: The film's success inspired imitators and martial arts clones, (Bruce Li, Bruce Le, Dragon Lee) but none could match the intensity and charisma of the original martial arts icon.

International Adaptations: From Remakes to Cultural Pride. Cultural Heritage: Bruce Lee's portrayal of Chen Zhen pays homage to traditional Chinese martial arts, highlighting China's cultural heritage.

Global Resurgence: "Fist of Fury" remakes and adaptations in various languages and countries continue to bring its themes and action-packed nature to new audiences.

Enduring Impact: Beyond Borders.
Cultural Phenomenon: "Fist of Fury" became a cultural phenomenon, symbolizing pride for the Chinese community worldwide and transcending language barriers.

Legacy Beyond Bruce Lee: The film's success paved the way for other Asian martial arts stars like Jackie Chan and Jet Li, inspiring a new generation of action film heroes.

Timeless Message: The film's theme of standing up against injustice continues to resonate, inspiring individuals to fight for what is right and symbolizing the strength of the human spirit.

Turning Point for Bruce Lee: "Fist of Fury" marked a turning point in Bruce Lee's career, solidifying his status as a martial arts legend and global superstar.

International superstar. His magnetic presence on screen and unparalleled martial arts skills made him a global icon. The legacy of "Fist of Fury" lives on, as it continues to be celebrated as a masterpiece of martial arts cinema and a testament to Bruce Lee's enduring legacy. The film's impact can still be felt today, inspiring new generations of martial arts enthusiasts and filmmakers.

In conclusion: Fist of Fury is a legendary martial arts film that has captivated audiences for decades with its thrilling action sequences, compelling storyline, and unforgettable characters; it has secured its place as a classic in the genre. Fist of Fury continues to leave a lasting impression on moviegoers worldwide continuing to bring new generations into discovering the on screen magic of Bruce lee.

BRUCE LEE COLUMN

REAL OR FAKE: CHINESE GUNG FU BY MICHAEL NESBITT

For many Bruce Lee collectors, one of the Holy Grail items of collecting is owning an original first edition copy of "Chinese Gung Fu: The Philosophical Art of Self-Defence", which was the only book Bruce Lee released during his lifetime. Unfortunately for collectors, there are many dangers and myths surrounding this elusive book, so for this month's Eastern Heroes Bruce Lee Column, we delve into the facts and give you tips on how to spot an authentic copy.

THE HISTORY OF THE BOOK

Martial Arts practitioner, teacher, author and publisher, James Yimm Lee, first met Bruce Lee in 1959, a meeting that would spawn a friendship that would last a lifetime. James, who was born and raised in Oakland California, and who had fought for the US Army during World War II, was a martial artist, who was famous for his Iron Palm. James would become quite an influential figure in Bruce Lee's life; he was the man who introduced Bruce to Ed Parker, the organiser of the Long Beach International Karate Championships. James was also present during the infamous fight between Bruce Lee and Wong Jack Man and would become one of only three certified 3rd rank instructors under Bruce Lee, the other two being Taky Kimura and Dan Inosanto. James, along with Bruce, was also the co-founder of the Jun Fan Gung Fu Institute in Oakland, where he taught Jun Fan Gung Fu in Bruce's absence. But more importantly, James was responsible for publishing Bruce Lee's first and only book. Not only was James Lee's publishing company, Oriental Books Sales, selling martial arts books from noted martial artists of the period, but he was also publishing, writing and selling his own books. It was during their first meeting that James had shown Bruce some of the books he had written and released, including Modern Kung Fu Karate books 1 and 2. Bruce was fascinated and explained to James his own ideas on releasing a book on his own Martial

Arts style of Wing Chun. With encouragement and help from James, Bruce Lee quickly began putting ideas together for the foundation of Chinese Gung Fu: The Philosophical Art of Self-Defence, a book that would not just focus on Martial arts techniques, but would also focus on the philosophical side of this ancient art.

With a number of his students in tow, including Taky Kimura and James DeMile, Bruce took photos of various fighting techniques, and once Bruce had all the written and photographic material together, he set off for Oakland to show James Lee. After many hours of formatting the layout, James took Bruce to the printing company he used in Berkeley, whereupon they

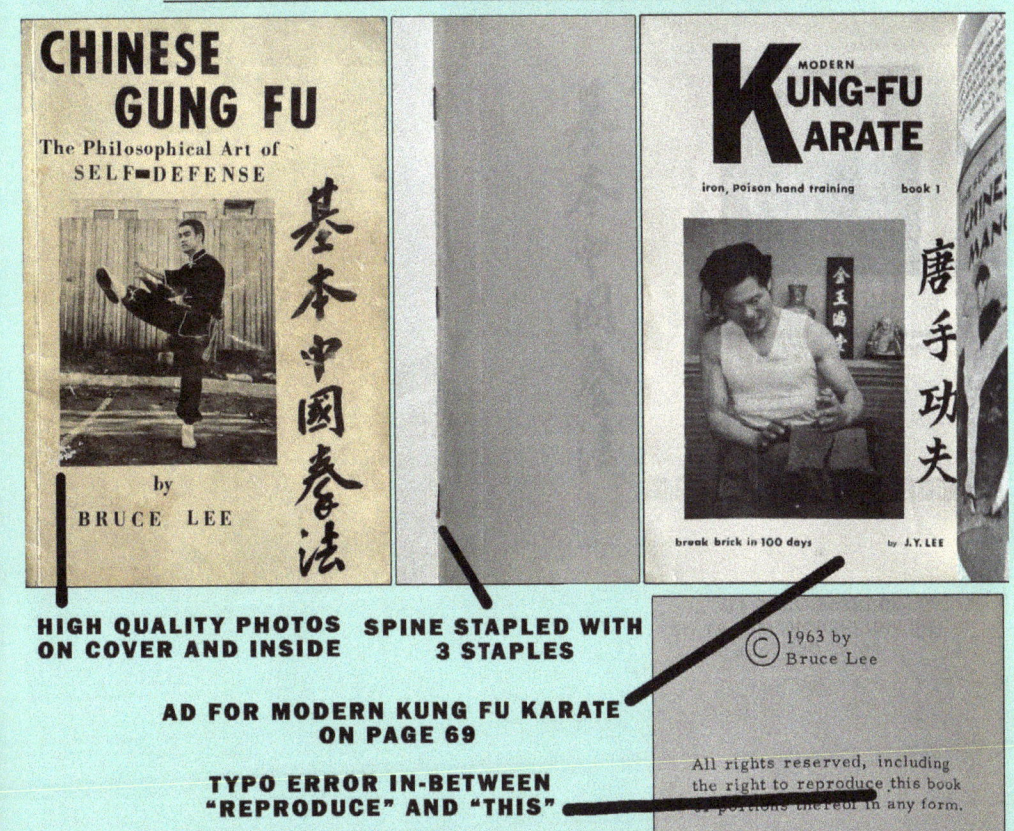

ORIGINAL FIRST EDITION FIRST PRINTING

- HIGH QUALITY PHOTOS ON COVER AND INSIDE
- SPINE STAPLED WITH 3 STAPLES
- AD FOR MODERN KUNG FU KARATE ON PAGE 69
- TYPO ERROR IN-BETWEEN "REPRODUCE" AND "THIS"

ORIGINAL FIRST EDITION SECOND PRINTING

- COVER SAME AS ORIGINAL, BUT DUST JACKET WITH GREEN HORNET TITLE (ADDED POST-1966)
- SPINE STAPLED WITH 2 STAPLES
- AD FOR TAO OF GUNG FU ON PAGE 69
- TYPO ERROR IN-BETWEEN "REPRODUCE" AND "THIS" REMOVED

showed the layouts to the printing manager. After agreeing to the price of $612 for 1500 copies of the book, the process of printing it was underway. In December 1963, Both James and Bruce drove to the printers to finally pick up Bruce's newly printed book.

VERSIONS OF THE BOOK

There were four official versions released of the book: 1st edition released by James Lee's Oakland Book Sales in 1963. 2nd edition released by OHARA Publications in 1987. 3rd edition released by O'Hara in 1988. 4th edition released by Black Belt Books in 2008. All three editions of the books are clearly marked, unfortunately during the 1980s; there were a number of badly published fake copies of the book being sold, which were sold as first edition copies from 1963. Luckily for Bruce Lee fans, there are several ways you can differentiate between an original and a fake copy.

HOW TO SPOT A FAKE

There are two different fake versions of the book.
1- The cover of the Fake 1 copy is normally bright yellow, whereas the Fake 2 is the same colour as the original, which is light beige in colour.
2- The Fake 1 version has a flat spine with no book title or author written on it, and the Fake 2 version has a stapled spine. The original first edition copy from 1963 has a flat spine, and has the title and author written on the spine, and is stapled together on the inside with the cover glued on.
3- The major difference between an original 1963 copy of the book, and the fake versions, are the photographs, the original has crystal clear photographs on the cover and inside, whereas the photographs in the fake copies are dark, blurry, and very low in quality.
(The Fake 1 version with the flat spine was made by Danny O'Connor of Oriental World Martial Arts Shop and was sold at the 1980 S.I.P. Bruce Lee Convention in the UK. The Fake 2 version with the stapled spine originated sometime in the

FAKE BOOK 1

YELLOW COVER NOT BEIGE

BLANK SPINE WITH NO TITLE

BAD QUALITY PHOTOS ON COVER AND INSIDE

1980s and was sold in numerous Chinatowns in America.)

TWO PRINTINGS OF THE 1st EDITION

There were at least two printings of the first edition. There is the first edition first printing from 1963, and it is generally acknowledged that there were other printings released shortly after the first one sold out. To capitalise on the release of The Green Hornet TV show, the post-1966 printings of the book usually came with a dust jacket that mentioned The Green Hornet TV show on the front. Both printings of the book have the same copyright page date; however, there are a couple of indicators to differentiate between the two.
1- In the first edition first printing copy of the book, just underneath the copyright date on the copyright page, there is a typo error in between the words "reproduce" and "this". The typo error looked like this "reproduce .this" The full stop should not be there, it should simply be "reproduce this". In the reprint, the mistake has been taken out and is no longer visible.
2- In the 1963 first edition of the book, on page 69 there is an ad for James Lee's book 'Modern Kung Fu Karate: Book 1', whereas in the second printing of the book, the advert on

FAKE BOOK 2

NO SPINE STAPLED

BAD QUALITY PHOTOS ON COVER AND INSIDE

page 69 has been changed, and is now an advert for Bruce Lee's 'Tao of Gung Fu' essay. 3- The first edition from 1963 has three staples inside holding the book together, whereas the second printing normally has two staples.

Chinese Gung Fu: The Philosophical Art of Self-Defence, was advertised for sale for around five years, and publicised in magazines such as Popular Science, Popular Mechanics, and various Martial Arts magazines in America. Nobody knows for sure how many first edition copies of the books were printed; however, it is generally considered around 600 of the first edition second printings were printed, with around 2000 copies printed all together, with at least 100 copies of the book mistakenly thrown away by Greglon Lee's friend, who stored them in his garage for him, and thought he didn't want them anymore. If you are lucky to find an authentic copy of Chinese Gung Fu, and you want to make sure it is authentic, or if you want to learn more about the book and James Lee, please visit the wonderful website set up by Steve Palmer:
https://bruceleechinesegungfubook.com.

MODERN KUNG FU KARATE BY JAMES LEE - BOOK 1 PART 1

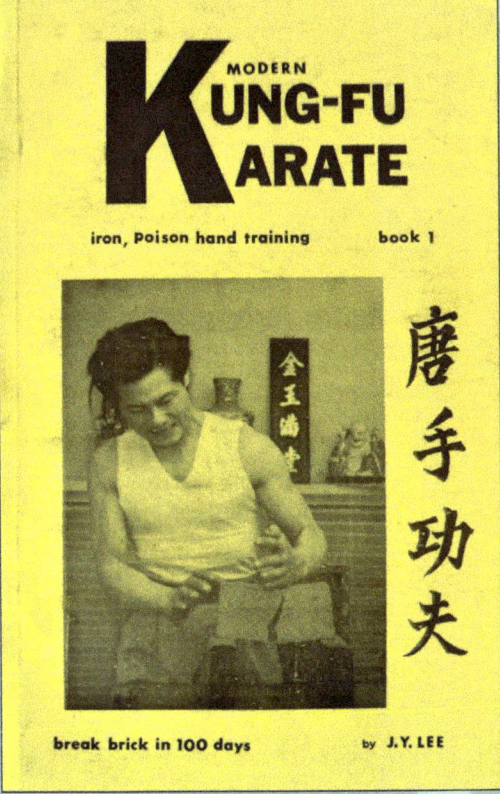

MODERN KUNG FU KARATE BY JAMES LEE - BOOK 1 PART 2

JAMES LEE AND HIS IRON PALM

PAGE 39 FIST OF FURY SPECIAL

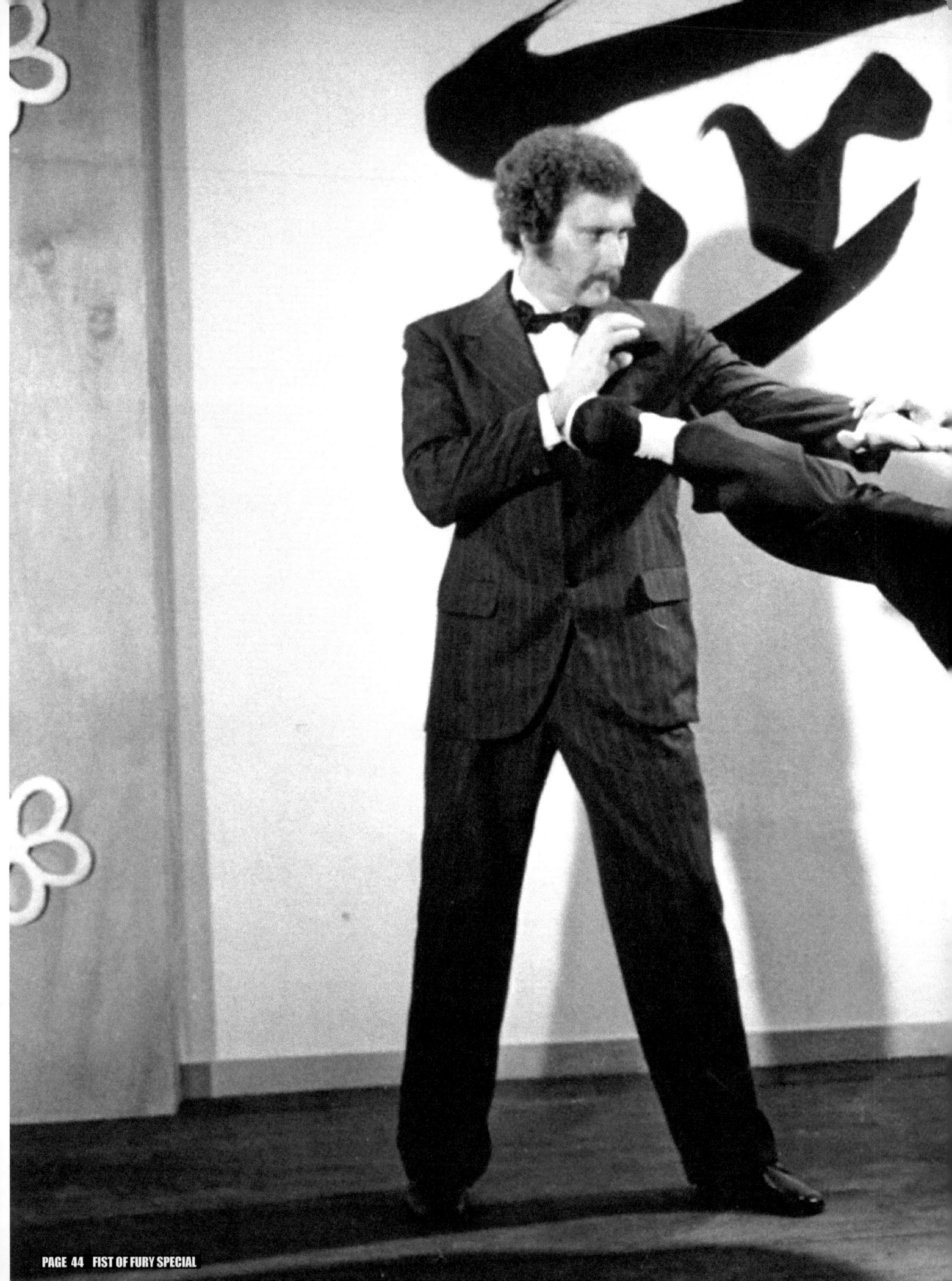

FIST OF FURY MEMORABILIA
FROM THOMAS GROSS

ADVERTISING

Brasil Press sheet

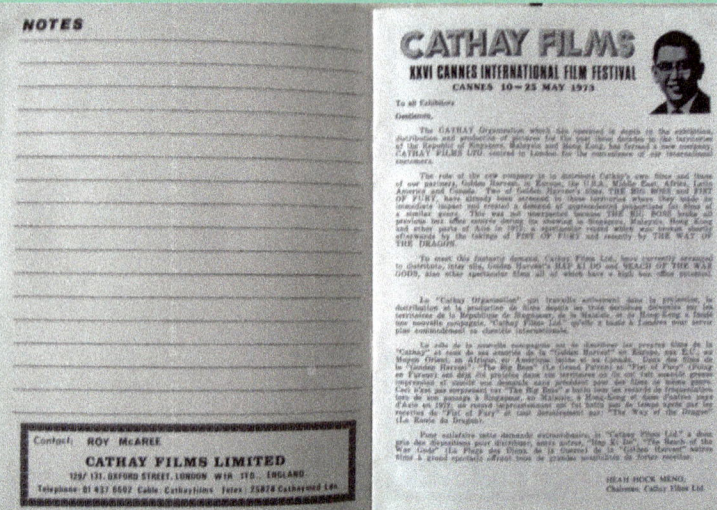

Cathay Booklet Cannes 1973

Brasil Press sheet

Cathay Booklet Cannes 1973

Cathay Booklet Cannes 1973

Denmark Press sheet

Denmark Press sheet

French matchbox - Rene Chateau

Todesgrüße aus Shanghai

Kamera: Chen Ching Chu
Musik: Joseph Koo
Schnitt: Chang Yao Chung
Produktion: Golden Harvest
Produzent: Raymond Chow
Buch und Regie: LO WEI

Mit Bruce Lee, Nora Miao, Maria Yi, Tien Feng, Huang Chung Hsin, Han Ying Chieh

Verleih: FILMZENTRUM

So hatte noch niemand Cheng gesehen, diesen eisernen Kämpfer mit knochenharten Fäusten.
Doch zu tief war Cheng vom Tode seines Lehrers Ho betroffen, der der Begründer der chinesischen Schule der Selbstverteidigungskünste und mehr noch, Chengs väterlicher Freund war.
Cheng ist in Trauer erstarrt. Aber er sinnt auf Rache. Dann er vermutet, daß die Angehörigen der rivalisierenden japanischen Schulvereinigung seinen Lehrer auf dem Gewissen haben. Indessen bringt ihm ein erster auf eigene Faust durchgeführter Rachezug keine Beweise für seine Verdächtigungen. Dagegen fordert der Lehrmeister der japanischen Schule, daß man ihm Cheng zur Bestrafung für seinen Rachekampf ausliefert. Während seiner Flucht vor den ständigen Bedrohungen und Nachstellungen findet Cheng handfeste Beweise für seinen Verdacht: Sein Lehrer Ho ist tatsächlich von den Japanern ermordet worden. In grenzenlosem Zorn nimmt er den gnadenlosen Kampf gegen eine Übermacht auf und vernichtet mit seinen Todesfäusten den japanischen Schulmeister, die tüchtigsten Schüler, darunter einen besonders gefährlichen russischen Kämpfer.
Chengs Rachedurst ist gestillt. Doch als er anschließend Shanghai verlassen will, muß er bei einem letzten Besuch in seiner alten Schule feststellen, daß alle seine Freunde ermordet worden sind. Während Cheng noch darüber nachsinnt, wie er reagieren soll, kommt der japanische Konsul zusammen mit dem Polizeichef, um Cheng festzunehmen. Cheng jedoch entflieht. Und seine Rache wird blutiger und furchtbarer, als seine Gegner es in ihren schlimmsten Träumen sich hatten vorstellen können...

Argentina Lobby cards

Australian Press Release

Australian Lobby Cards

Chen of murdering the Japanese Headmaster. Chen makes a hasty escape. He then appears on the roof of the school and the film comes to a startling climax.

International cast of Europe's top Kung Fu Experts.

CREDITS

Directed and Written by
BRUCE LEE

ACCESSORIES

DAYBILLS
SLIDES
PRESS SHEETS
TRAILERS

RUNNING TIME 103 min.

including a famed Russian exponent of the martial arts.

Satisfied this is revenge enough Chen decides to leave Shanghai he then finds that all his old school friends have been mysteriously massacred. While planning his next action the Japanese Consul arrives with the Chief of Police and accuses

LENGTH 2826 m.

Italian Newspaper adverts - March 1973

Newspaper Advert - New York - 1972

UFA Super 8 Flyer Germany 1978

Newspaper Advert - Hong Kong

Video Flyer French Rene Chateau

Newspaper Advert - USA

FRENCH LOBBY CARDS - FIRST RELEASE

FRENCH SECOND RELEASE
RENE CHATEUA

PAGE 63 FIST OF FURY SPECIAL

GERMAN LOBBY CARDS - FIRST RELEASE

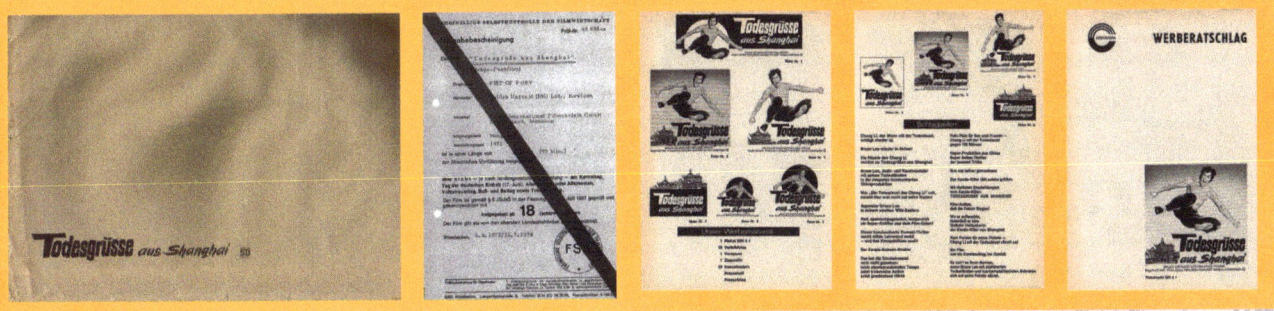

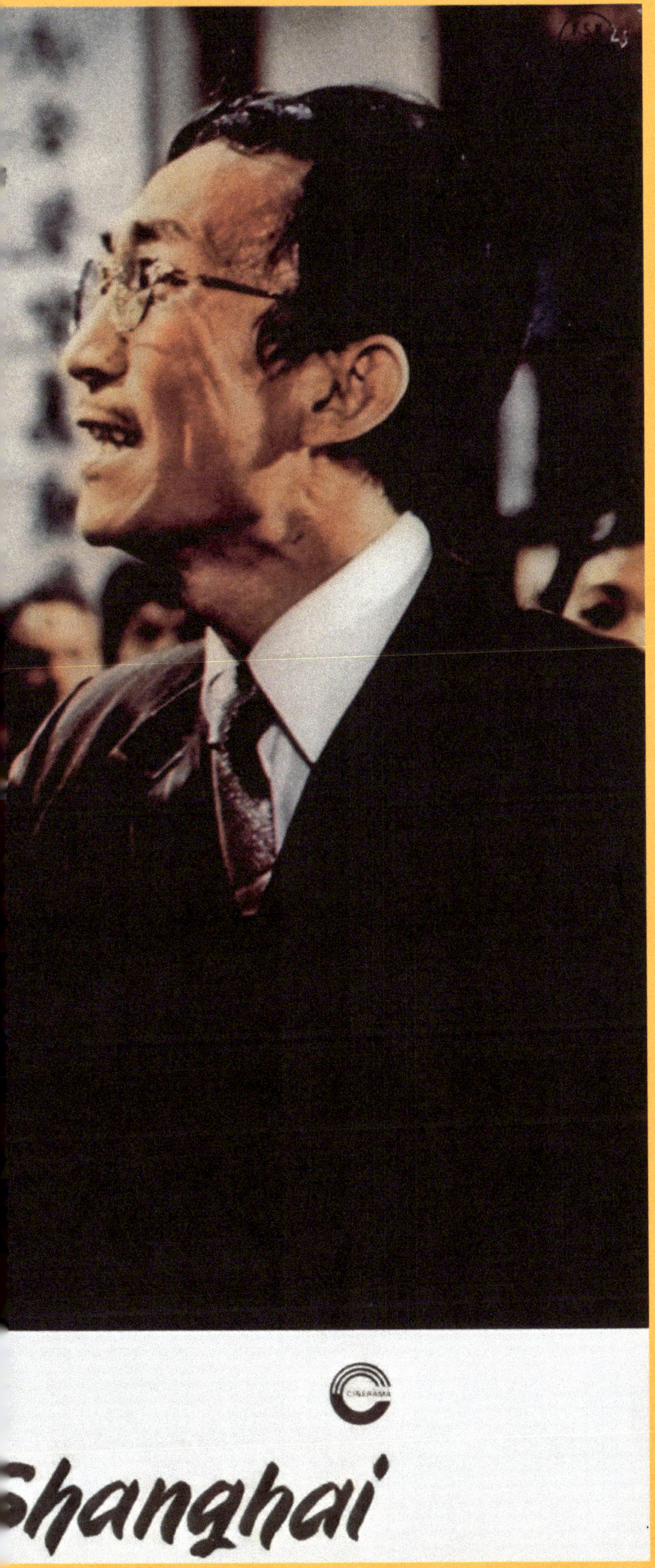

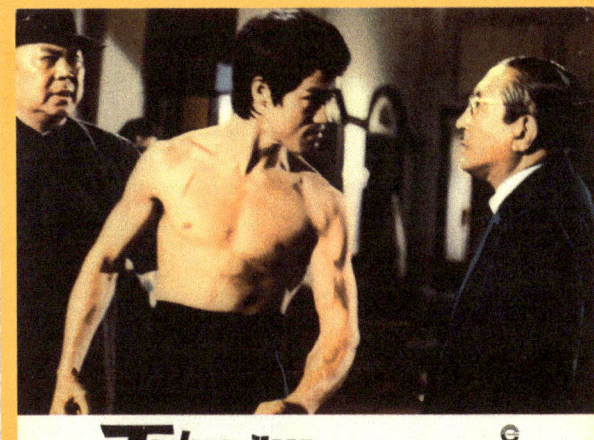

CINERAMA
Shanghai

Todesgrüsse aus Shanghai

Todesgrüsse aus Shanghai

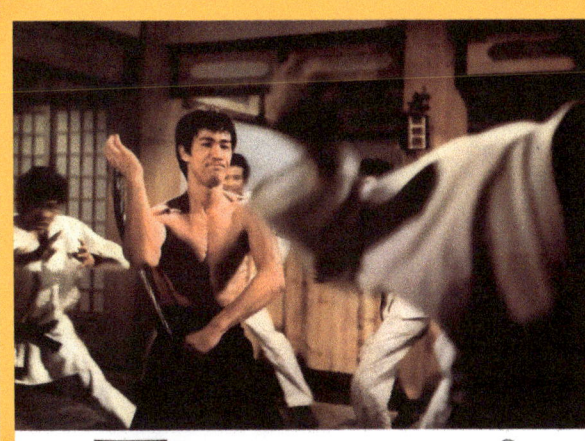

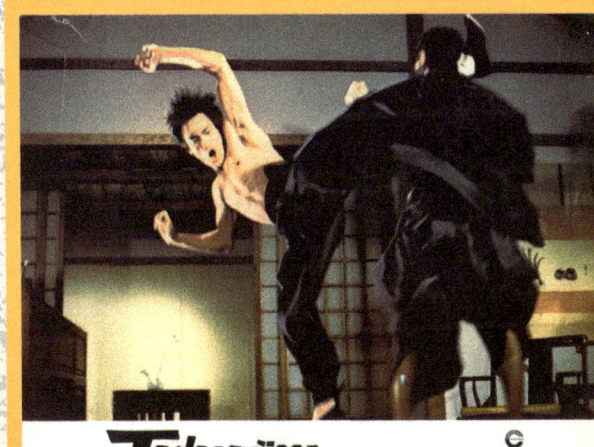

Todesgrüsse aus Shanghai

HONG KONG 1980'S RELEASE

Hong Kong poster 1980's

Hong Kong International poster 1980's

AUSTRALIA RELEASES

Hong Kong (first release)

Hong Kong (first release)

JEFF CHINN

THE GATEKEEPER OF THE BRUCE LEE LEGACY (PART 2)
By Rick Baker and Simon Pritchard

In Volume 2, Issue 3 of the Bruce Lee special, Jeff Chinn graciously dedicated some time to discuss his esteemed Bruce Lee collection. The conversation spanned two interviews, and instead of condensing it, we presented it as a two-part special. If you missed the first part, you can locate it in Volume 2, Issue No. 3 — it's certainly worth the read, especially if you're a Bruce Lee memorabilia collector.

RB: You've met quite a few collectors in your time, who's a couple of the people that you rate as a collector?

JC: I consider Perry Lee my senior in terms of Bruce Lee collecting because he actually did start during the Green Hornet days and Perry is in his mid-70s now. So it kind of makes sense that he was old enough during the Green Hornet that he remembers that was Bruce Lee and to my knowledge, he's the only major collector to have met Bruce Lee in person twice. Including once when Bruce Lee was demonstrating at a high school in Seattle. He also has a good relationship with Shannon and Linda and he has also done many projects on Bruce Lee.

RB: Was he lucky enough to take a photograph? Does he have that immortal photograph that we all wish we had?

JC: No, he met Bruce Lee back in 1962. So the story in a nutshell is that Bruce came to Perry's high school and he demonstrated his Chinese Kung Fu. But for some reason, I don't know if Bruce did it on purpose but Bruce Lee dressed up in a suit and tie with glasses and he kind of looked like a typical so-and-so.

Perry noticed that people in the audience were kind of just staring at him. You know, what are you doing? Kind of dancing around with these moves or whatever. So what Bruce did was he asked the audience who the toughest member of the high school was. So this big black guy named Carl, I think it was Carl Wood. So Carl Wood went up on stage with Bruce and then Bruce simply asked Carl, I want you to hit me. So of course, Carl tried to punch him and then Bruce blocked it and had a fist right in front of Carl's face and the crowd was rooting for Carl.

Some of them were chanting "Knock off that China man's head off" or whatever. So, of course, Carl tried, but then Bruce would trap him, you know and make fun, like tapping on the top of his head and saying "knock, knock" or whatever. Bruce totally embarrassed that guy.

Perry was so impressed that he went up to Bruce afterwards and then the first question that Bruce asked Perry was "Are you Chinese?" as most of the audience were not. Perry said yes and then they were just talking with each other.

Here's the biggest blunder of Perry's Bruce Lee collecting life is that Bruce Lee asked Perry "Would you like to join my school?" And then Perry thinks, so your school's here, so I would have to take this bus transfer to this bus and I don't know if my Mom and Dad are going to let me.... So he politely declined.

The thing is, hindsight's a fantastic thing, isn't it?

RB: Yes, and we're still talking about it now, 50 years on. What sort of items does Perry have?

JC: One thing that stands out is that you know he's connected with a lot of people in Seattle, so he was good friends with the son of Ruby Chow. You know, Ruby Chow's the restaurant owner where Bruce Lee worked as a waiter and stayed. When Bruce Lee had left Seattle to move to Oakland, Ruby Chow's son asked Perry "Hey, you know that Bruce Lee guy left kind of in a hurry, he left a bunch of stuff in his room. Would you like to check it out?"

So Perry checked it out and saw, in particular, this thing that looked like a head that was made out of steel or iron and black electrical tape, and it was on this wooden plank or whatever. So apparently James Lee from Oakland had made this for Bruce because it was the typical James Lee trademark, you know, with the springs and this and that. Perry asked Ruby Chow's son whether he wanted it and he said no. So, Perry took it.

RB: Is this something that has been displayed or is it one of those items that has never seen the light of day?

JC: Perry has loaned it to the Hong Kong Museum.

RB: The one thing I enjoyed about that exhibition the first time I went was the documentary that they were screening which you could never see outside the museum; I thought it was an excellent documentary.

JL: The people that have gone to the museum have asked me "Since you loaned it to the museum, did they give you a DVD copy or whatever?" The answer is no, they're very private with that documentary. I guess in their contract that to do it is only exclusive to the museum itself and you have to go to the museum to see it. But I do agree with you that it's an excellent documentary. To be honest, it is the only Bruce documentary that brought tears to my eyes at the end.

RB: I was lucky enough to screen The Orphan just a few years ago and it was very difficult to get. It would be nice to see a DVD or something. Have you seen it and do you know if there is a copy of it out there?

JC: Yeah, but a couple of years ago, they had a special screening at the Great Star

Theatre in Star School, Chinatown. It was a very rare screening and they were so strict that they had two security guards sitting to the left and right of the screen and if they saw anyone with a light on on their cell phone trying to film it, they just ushered them out of the theatre.

RB: What is in Perry's collection? Is it specific to magazines or posters? or miscellaneous?

JC: He collects almost everything. But I think another highlight is that he's probably got the largest Bruce Lee business card collection. I mean he's got like, maybe 90% of them including the gold prototype one where you don't see the jaggedly symbol, you see like a little circle. Perry has three autographs; a special one in particular was this fan in Portland who attended one of those Kato signings. I'm sure you've seen pictures of Bruce's Kato signing for those little kids. Perry called one of those little kids and he still had the autograph.

So because Seattle was right next to Portland, Perry drove over there and you know, of course, there's no COA or whatever, but as soon as Perry saw it, he knew that it was the real deal.

RB: Perry seems quite reclusive. He's never interviewed I believe. Has he ever talked about his collection?

JC: Yeah. All right, so here's a story that probably neither of you know, a lot of people don't. In 2003 he opened up a major Bruce Lee Museum in Seattle and it was also used to raise money for the Chinatown community. Unfortunately, Perry did not ask Shannon in the beginning for permission. His lawyers and her lawyers spent a similar year fighting back

said deflated Perry, She looked around and said "what the fuck is this?"

Ironically, after it was shut, Perry got a letter from Shannon saying, she had changed her mind and would like to work with them. But it was too late.

RB: The other collector you spoke about is Yuri Nakamura.

JC: Yes, Yuri has such a gigantic collection. So at least Perry and I centralised our Bruce Lee Museum into one big room. Yuri Nakamura has it in his living room, dining room, hallway, and bedroom. I mean, it's like taking over his whole apartment.

He opened up a lot of exhibitions in Japan, to the point that in Japan he was like a Rockstar in terms of Bruce Lee exhibitions, whatever and I would call him like a protégé of Dan Inosanto. But something happened within the last five years or so that Yuri just dropped off the face of the Earth.

Yuri and I have put on several exhibitions; did you Bruce wrote a script for himself for the Green Hornet? it is called the Dragon from the East. Shannon loaned us the actual script. She said "This is my father" Because of the lack of dialogue and screen time or whatever, Bruce got frustrated and wrote out his script, which of course included a lot of dialogue for Kato, a lot of scenes with him and Shannon told me that, of course, when the producer or the director got the script it probably went in the trash. The script was dated 1966.

RB: What's the most obscure item you own?

JC: Yeah. Well, there's one thing that that I kept, or I took, when they tore down the Chinese hospital back in 2000, my wife and I went to Chinatown every other week and we would try to salvage pieces from the Chinese hospital and the sad part is, is that my wife and I were the only people there.

They were just dumping everything, so I managed to get some nice pieces to make a Long story short, I actually got the windows right above where Bruce Lee was. Yes, yes, the actual windows from the Chinese hospital.

When they take that wrecking ball and destroy the building, they, of course, have to take down all the windows because they don't want the glass to be flying all over the place. So it's up to the construction people to take out each window individually. This one construction worker, whom I got a friendship with, decided to take a pair of windows for himself for a project, but when he found out that the windows were just too large and too heavy for the project, he asked me if I wanted them, so I said yes. I had to go right away to the hospital because he said I was hiding them from my supervisor. If

you want them, you, you gotta come now.

RB: What do you do with those?

JC: I know, 'cause they're so huge and heavy that I just have them on the side of my display room and to protect them, I have put like cardboard above them. People say, "Why don't you repaint them?", "Why don't you clean the glass with....?" no, no no no no.

SP: What influence did Bruce Lee have on your childhood?

JC: I need to share, this is what what keeps me going.

I was born in the same hospital as Bruce Lee, but because of all the negative stereotypes in movies, TV and whatnot, I was very ashamed of my Chinese heritage, so I never told any of my friends that I was born in Chinatown.

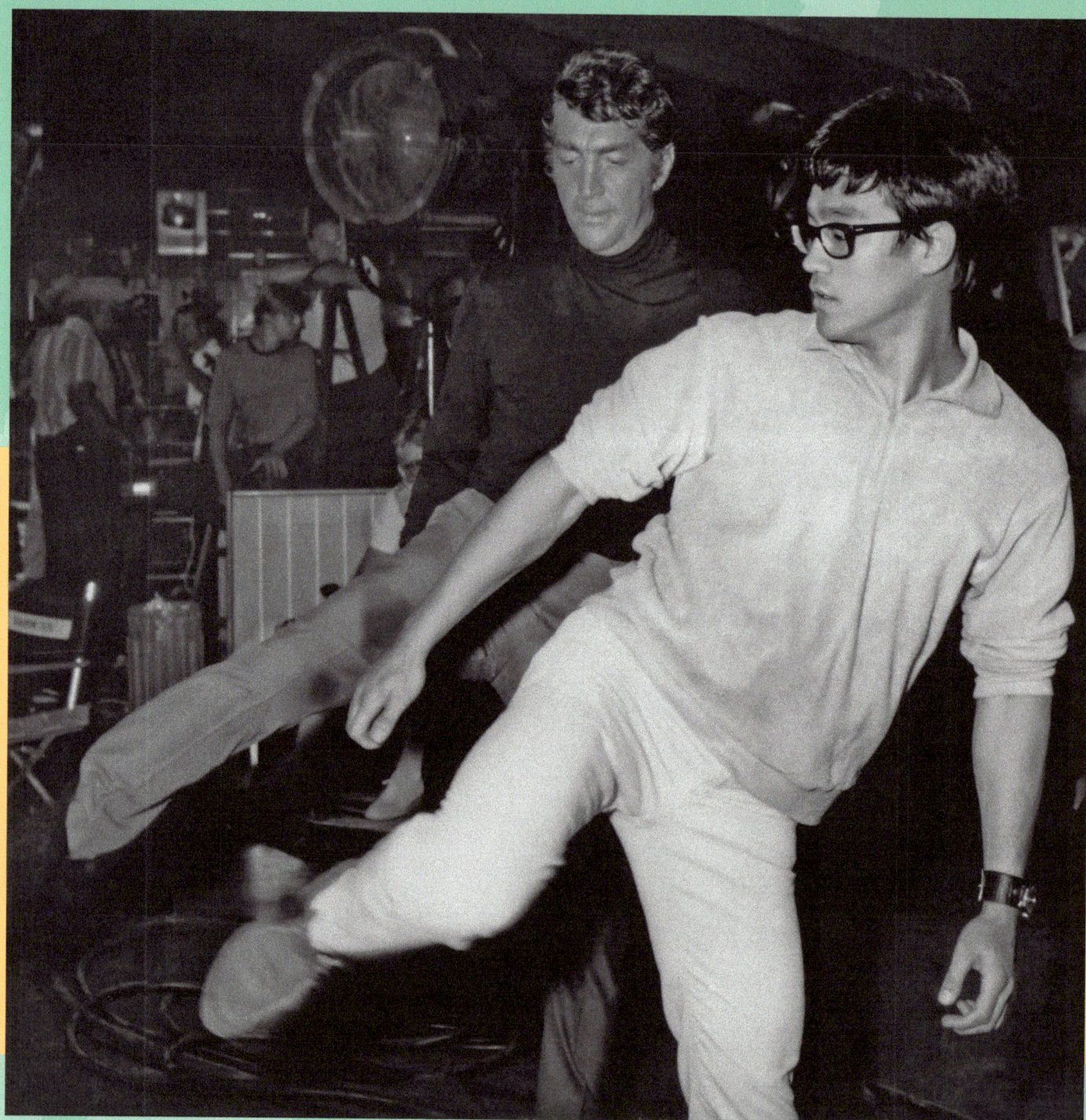

Fast forward to seeing my first movie, "The Big Boss", after I came home, my Mom sat me down in the kitchen and said, "Jeff, I'm going to tell you something that you're going to like". And I said, "What you gonna give me a raise in my allowance?" She said "no, no", she said "Did you realise that you and Bruce were born in the same hospital?

I fell out of my chair. Got back up and I said, "wait till I go back to school". I now bragged to all my friends that I was born in the same hospital as Bruce Lee. So it shows a whole 360-degree change in attitude thanks to one movie and one man.

So, because I'm sharing about my childhood, I need to share one extremely memorable moment from the 6th grade. so, "Fist of Fury" came out on the Friday. My Dad took me to see the movie on Saturday. When I went back to school on Monday, all my non-Chinese friends were looking at the Chinese a little differently.

We were going to play Kickball, and the Asians or the Chinese were usually picked last because of the negative stereotype that Asians are usually smaller and perceived as weaklings. The two Caucasian team captains were whispering to each other and said "Hey Jeff, we want to ask you something" I said, "Hey, what do you want?" They said "We just saw that movie "Fist of Fury with that guy named Bruce Lee. We saw Bruce Lee kick a guy right through the wall. Can you Chinese actually do that?" So I said "Uh-huh".

As you know, Simon, sometimes perception is stronger than reality. Yeah, but it was something very memorable because what I'm trying to say in a nutshell is being relatively invisible on Friday and then being greatly noticed on Monday, which is like overnight, all thanks to one movie and again, one man.

I grew up in San Francisco, So in 1974, my dad told us that we had to move and because we needed a bigger house, my brother, my sister and I, were sharing one bedroom, it was getting kind of crowded. It wasn't until the first day of the 8th grade. Where I was in total shock. Where's all the Chinese? Where's all the Asians? So I shockingly found out that I was the only Chinese in my 8th grade class.

As a result, I got picked on, I got called every racial slur in the book and I'm pretty sure that you know, back in the old days we didn't have anti-bullying laws. We didn't have school counsellors that could help me out. So basically, I was on my own in the beginning.

I would hide in the library because bullies tend not to want to step foot into libraries, but that that could only last for so long. My Mom started to notice whenever I would eat, I'd have an extremely severe stomach pain. So she took me to the doctor, and then the doctor was quite shocked. He had never seen anyone so young, I was only 13, and I had a bleeding ulcer from holding and all that stress. The acid in my stomach was churning and causing bleeding. So as a result, I had to go on a very strict diet for a year. Everything I ate was plain and before each meal, I had to coat my stomach with this thick, nasty liquid that coated my stomach.

OK, so one day I was in my bedroom, and I only had one Bruce Lee poster that was hanging on the wall, I looked at the poster and I was crying and it was almost like Bruce Lee was speaking to me, saying "OK Jeff, because I, Bruce Lee, am Chinese American. I, Bruce Lee, have probably faced even more racism than you". And I looked. At the poster, I said, "Listen, Bruce, this is probably the darkest period of my life and I'm really gonna need your help. And if you help me, I'm going to pay you back Monday."

And that's why I'm doing what I'm doing now, to keep the life and legacy of Bruce Lee alive, because it's my way of paying him back. I volunteer at the museum every Wednesday and Saturday to give full personal tours. Of course, because I'm retired now, I'll get tired because there are so many people. So even though I'm tired and whatever. I have to keep my end of the bargain.

SP: You are also strong and physically fit, what's your routine? when did this start?

JC: in 1978, I read an issue of Fighting Stars magazine, which I'm sure you're very familiar

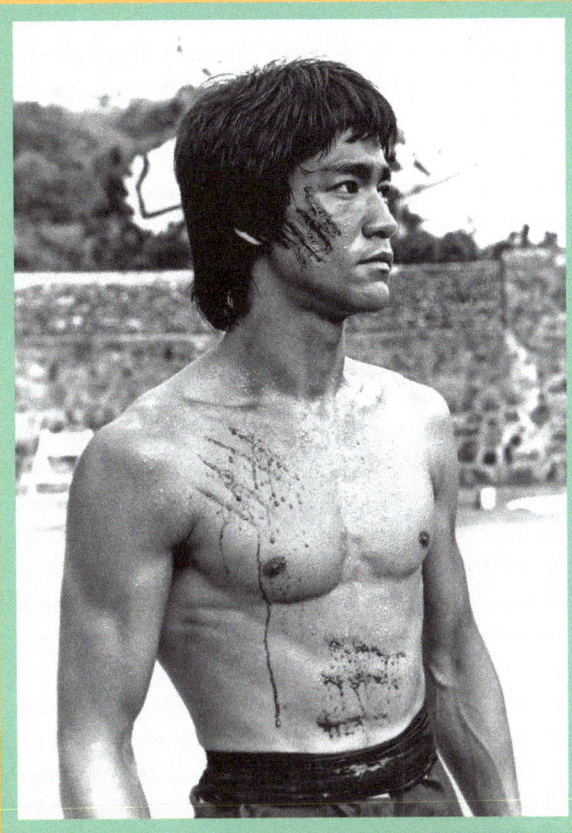

with. So that kind of puts me as a junior in high school, so I was about 17 years old. There was one quote from Bruce Lee that has resonated with me. Bruce Lee in the article said that I want to be the strongest and fittest 50-year-old in the entire world. So even though I was young, I knew that Bruce Lee would never be able to reach that goal because he died at the age of 30. I thought Alright, Bruce, in my way of paying you back, I'm going to try to do what you could never reach do. So I kept in shape, working out and everything. When I hit 50, I said OK, OK looks pretty good, I'm strong. But when I hit 60, Then it's like, you know, then things start to hurt, ache, but that's a progression of the human body.

Mentally you have to remind yourself that 60 is a new 50, right? Just sometimes people think, OK, I'm 40, I can't move around any more, you know, it takes some effort. Sometimes it gets boring and a lot of people just want the easy way of doing it. So there's one thing that I do religiously. When I hit 60, although I cannot exercise as much as I used to do, there is one exercise that I do twice a week. Every Wednesday and every Sunday. 12 consecutive pull-ups.

People ask me why 12. because I was 12 years old when I saw my first Bruce Lee movie. And sometimes I'm like at 10 and I'm just like, hang in there and then I said, OK, one more for Bruce, and then one last one. As you get older, you get heavier. So of course, pull-ups get tougher and tougher and that's why I spread it out from Wednesday to Sunday because it it gives me some rest.

Some people might call me crazy or whatever, but the two most famous muscles of Bruce Lee were his forearms and his lats. So when you do pull-ups, you're you're working

two basic muscles. It's the lats and it's the forearms. My lats used to be huge, but less now through age, but you know that's my way of just honouring Bruce and mainly maintaining my physique. I don't want people to look at me and go, "You claim to be a Bruce Lee fan. Well, you sure look like you're out of shape" or whatever.

SP: You were also the Contributing Editor for Inside Kung Fu magazine, can you tell us about that?

JC: OK. Yeah. So I did that for seven years, I mean you you guys know that to write something bimonthly or regularly, it gets kind of tiresome or frustrating because you have to keep up the quality of the subject matter.

During these seven years were some of the biggest fights between me and my wife because she was my editor then. In 2002, I got the Inside 'Kung Fu Hall of Fame Writer of the year award which was a big honour and I dedicated half of the honour to my wife.

Shockingly I got fired by Inside Kung Fu that same year. Not because of the quality of my writing. It was because at that time Shannon had a team of lawyers and was going through everyone and saying you can no longer use the image of Bruce Lee, say his name, whatever, without paying and of course, you know, magazines do not make any money. We're there just to promote people.

So they said, OK, we're going to stop. Stop your column. Whatever, but it was a blessing in disguise. To, be honest, Simon, since that day that I got cut by Inside Kung Fu, I do not want to write for any magazines because I got so burned out. The only time that I wrote something was the obituary for Allen Joe and George Lee. Because you know, they they they're very special friends. But I get asked by all these people and I just don't know whether to do it

3 or 4 Bruce Lee vintage magazines. Would you want them?" I said "Yeah, of course" He then said, "Well, can you come on over to Chinatown, and I'll give them to you".

So when I went there, of course, I asked "Does your uncle have anything else?" He said. "Well, here's three boxes full of magazines that that we're that were going to dump". And I replied, "Can I look through those?" I mean he had Golden Harvest Movie News from Issue #1, the complete set. My friend had just pulled out the Bruce Lee ones on the cover. I asked whether I could have them all, and he agreed, so I grabbed all the crates of magazines. I mean, you know, you don't find stuff like that in at at at the flea market.

SP: Is there anything else you would like to add?

JC: I'm very blessed that my wife let me have the biggest room in the entire house dedicated to Bruce Lee. I'm very lucky that she has fully supported me throughout this entire process. I had told you both that she was sitting next to me when I bid for the blue suit. She didn't, you know, take out a knife and slit my throat or whatever! So it helps that you have a spouse that you know is very supportive of what you do. You know just don't step over the line so to speak.

RB: We both thank you for your time and speak soon.

again. I also fear my wife as well, so let's see.

SP: You knew Allen Joe? That's cool, do you have any stories?

JC: Allen Joe! Yeah, he's the person who introduced Bruce Lee to bodybuilding, and that was very important to Bruce's life because Bruce became like a walking Grey's Anatomy chart. When Alan passed away, I got many of the weights that Allen and Bruce had trained on. Allen initially became Bruce's personal trainer, Bruce didn't have his own weight set, so Bruce would go over to Allen's house and they would work out.

I mean these these are like really old-looking. A little bit rusty or whatever, but it probably has all Bruce's DNA on it and of course the weight bench as well.

I'm running out of room because I have the hospital windows and now I have the whole rack of weights and the weight bench.

SP: You have a library worth of magazines, how did you accumulate so many?

JC: I have been lucky. One time, my friend was a caretaker of his uncle, or whatever; when the uncle passed away, he had this small apartment with tonnes of stuff. He said Jeff "I found like

JOHN NEGRON'S MEMORABILIA
VIDEO / DVD & SOUNDTRACKS

PAGE 89 FIST OF FURY SPECIAL

SPECIAL
WIDE SCREEN
EDITION
THE
DEADLIEST
ART
The Best of the Martial Arts Films
Featuring
Bruce Lee, Jackie Chan
Sho Kosugi and Cynthia Rothrock
LaserDisc
LASER DISC
FOX VIDEO
Extended Play
digital sound

WORLD OF
BRUCE
LEE

Today's Movie Hit Themes
WIDE DELUXE 2500

精
武
门
FIST OF
FURY

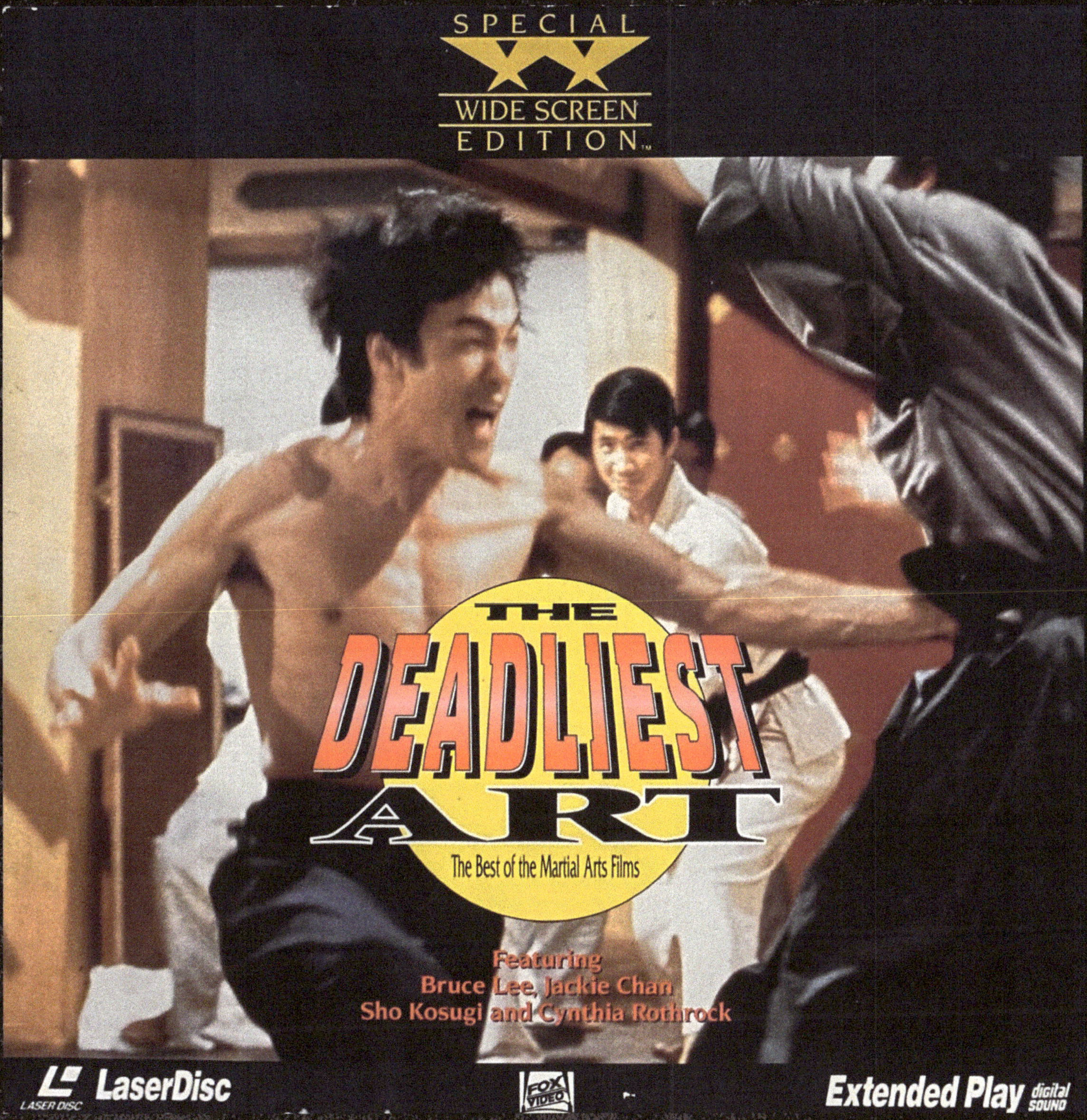

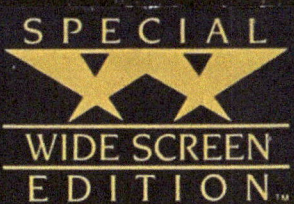

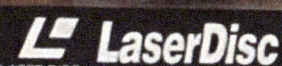

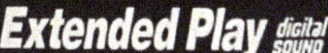

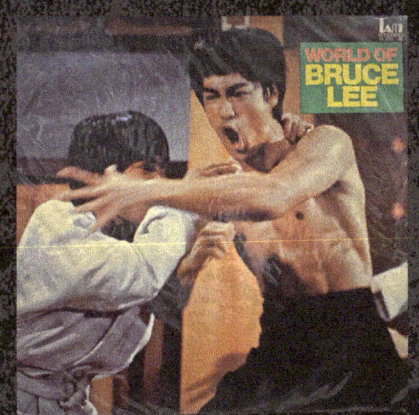

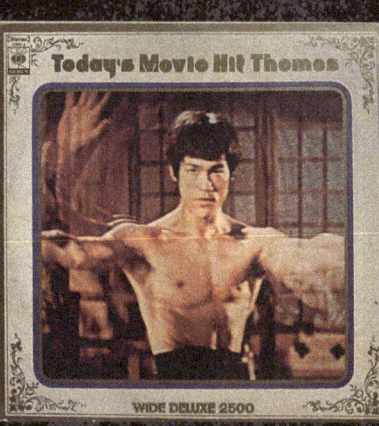

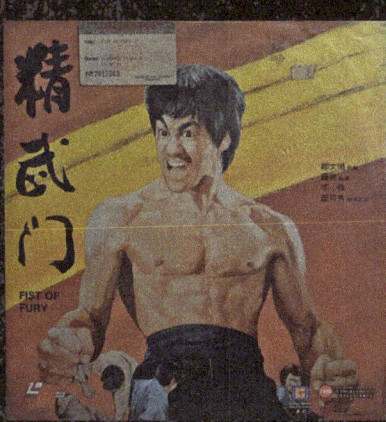

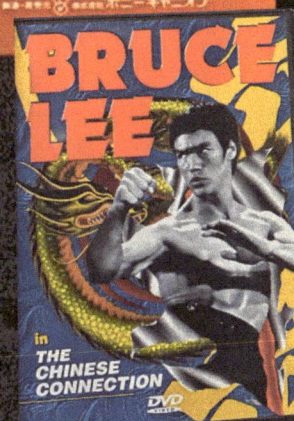
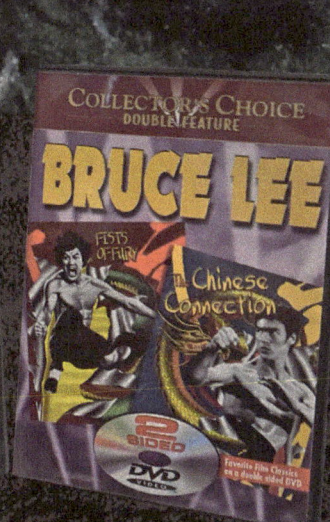
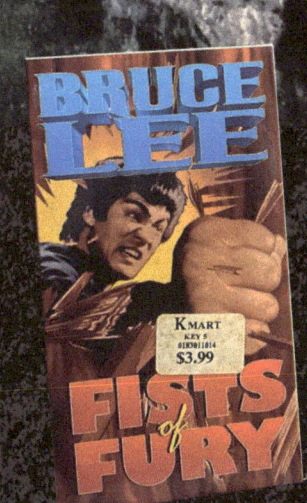

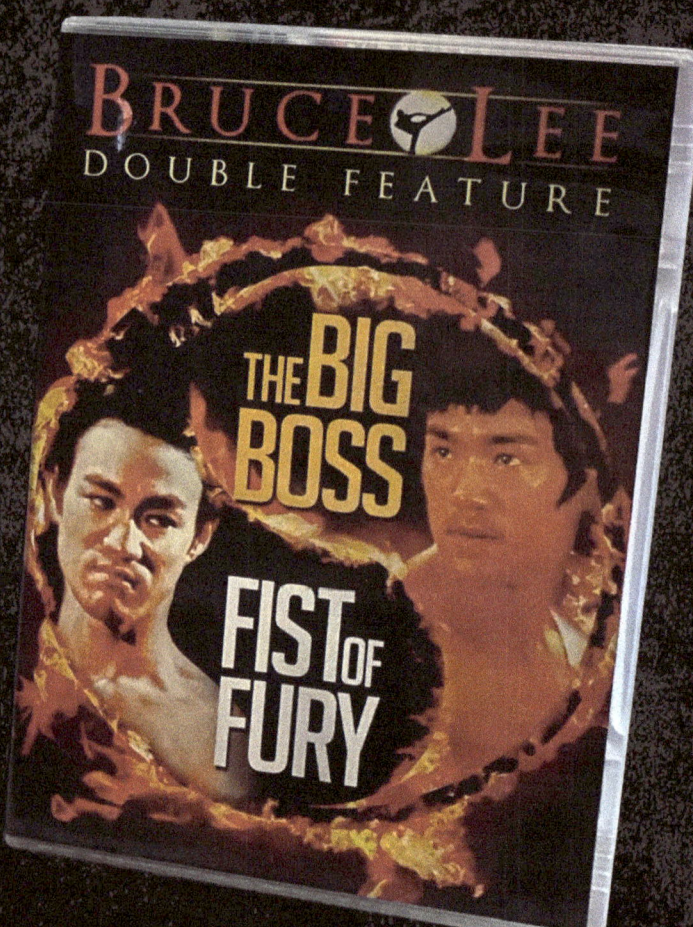

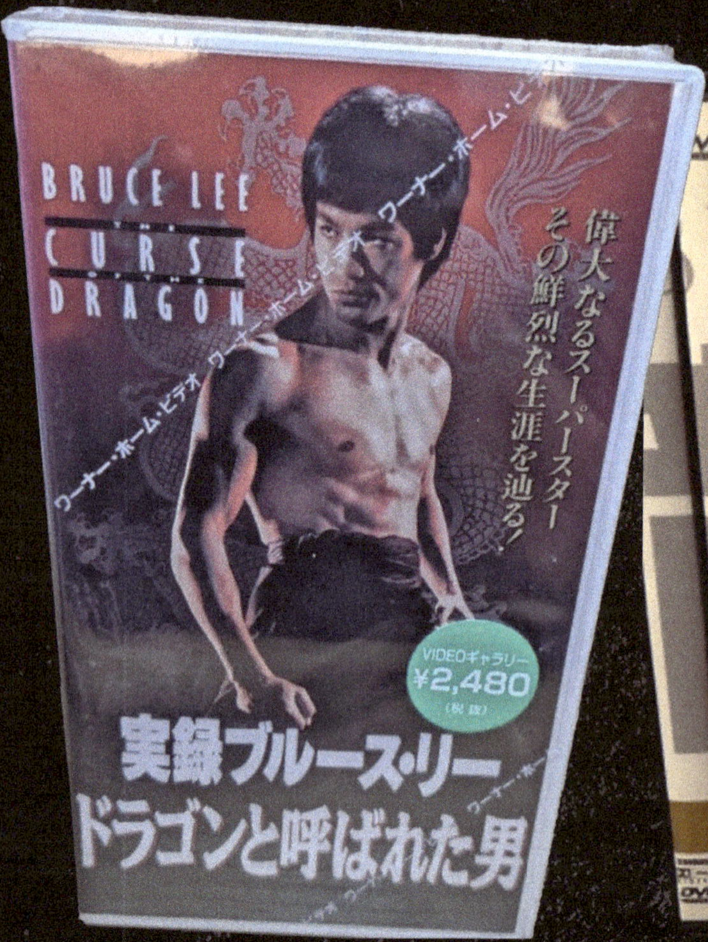

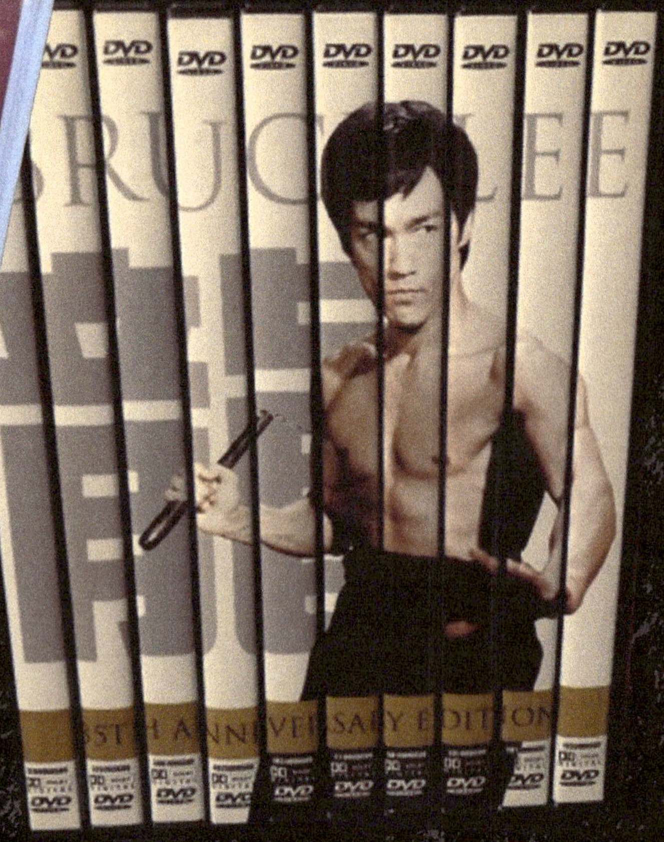

MAGAZINES & BOOKS

BRUCE LEE

HIS UNKNOWNS IN MARTIAL ARTS LEARNING

With a Bruce Lee autographed photo

BRUCE LEE HAD TEN MASTERS

BRUCE'S JKD CLUBBING METHOD

50 YEARS OF BRUCE LEE
REMEMBERING THE LEGEND

compiled and edited by
VINCENT CHUNG

BRUCE LEE
An Enduring Legacy at 50

compiled by
VINCENT CHUNG
edited and illustrated by
SIEWLAM CHONG

月刊秘伝 12

空前絶後のアクション・ヒーローにして真の武術家、ブルース・リーの深奥

武道・武術の秘伝に迫る
THE HIDEN BUDO & BUJUTSU

◎田村信喜先生追悼
　永遠なる"合気道の志"
◎萩原幸之助 短期集中連載！
　靭術とは何か？

2010 DEC.

ブルース・リーファン垂涎
膨大な未公開写真を含んだ
フォト・コレクションほか
豪華グッズ プレゼント！

1940年11月、"東洋の龍"が生まれた。

特集
生誕70周年記念公開
李小龍秘伝降臨
武人ブルース・リーの新事実発掘！
ジークンドー"5WAYS OF ATTACK"の秘密　ブルース・リーと日本武術

PAGE 102 FIST OF FURY SPECIAL

REMINISCENCE OF BRUCE LEE

by Wong Shun-leung

First hand information!
UNKNOWN ANECDOTES!

*Written by Bruce Lee's fellow-learner
Who taught him Kung Fu,*

**WONG SHUN LEUNG
RECALLS BRUCE LEE'S NAUGHTY DEEDS**

A Bruce Lee autographed photo included!

BRUCE LEE'S TRAINING METHODS

PAGE 105 FIST OF FURY SPECIAL

BUSHIDO

THE MARTIAL ART MAGAZINE   M.C.(P) 429/73

武士道

AT THE BUDOKAN
EXIT OF A SUPERSTAR
THE LADY GENERAL
FACTS AND FANTASY
BRUCE LEE AS I SEE HIM

$1

COPYRIGHT RESERVED

4

BUSHIDO

THE MARTIAL ARTS MAGAZINE M.C. (P) 96/74   KDN 7922

$2   COPYRIGHTS RESERVED   12

PAGE 107 FIST OF FURY SPECIAL

REVISTA BRUCE LEE

Nº 22 SEPTIEMBRE – AÑO III – 200 Pts. (IVA incluido)

PAGE 115 FIST OF FURY SPECIAL

BRUCE LEE
& JKD MAGAZINE

NO. 3

OPEN UP
BRUCE LEE'S
TRAINING ROOM

GIANT BRUCE LEE POSTER INSIDE

SKILLS! SKILLS!! SKILLS!!!
JEET-KUNE-DO WINS WITH SKILLS!

PAGE 118 FIST OF FURY SPECIAL

FIGHTERS' MONTHLY

50p
Vol 1 No 3

THE MAGAZINE FOR THE TRUE MARTIAL ARTS ENTHUSIAST

BRUCE LEE'S FIST OF FURY is back!

INOSANTO – His way

PLUS Photo Reports Shorinji Kempo and MONKEY BOXING

MEIJI SUZUKI KU SHANKU KATA

PAGE 119 FIST OF FURY SPECIAL

BRUCE LEE

THE LIFE • THE LEGACY • THE LEGEND

POSTER MAGAZINE / ISSUE 7

GBP £14.99 / USD $19.99

THE MAN BEHIND THE LEGEND

HOW **BRUCE LEE** AND **RAYMOND CHOW** REVOLUTIONIZED THE MARTIAL ARTS MOVIE INDUSTRY

FEATURING AN EXCLUSIVE INTERVIEW WITH ROBERTA CHOW

KUDOS MEMORABILIA

www.ingramcontent.com/pod-product-compliance
Lightning Source LLC
Chambersburg PA
CBHW061125170426
43209CB00013B/1672